TEEN
SURVIVAL
GUIDE

W9-DEM-912

SURVIVING
A FIRST DATE

TAYLOR MORRIS

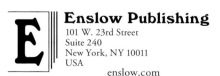

Enslow Publishing
101 W. 23rd Street
Suite 240
New York, NY 10011
USA

enslow.com

Published in 2018 by Enslow Publishing, LLC.
101 W. 23rd Street, Suite 240, New York, NY 10011

Library of Congress Cataloging-in-Publication Data

Names: Morris, Taylor, author.
Title: Surviving a first date / by Taylor Morris.
Description: New York : Enslow Publishing, 2018. | Series: Teen survival guide | Includes bibliographical references and index. | Audience: Grades 7–12.
Identifiers: LCCN 2017015073| ISBN 9780766091917 (library bound) | ISBN 9780766093614 (pbk.) | ISBN 9780766093621 (6 pack)
Subjects: LCSH: Dating (Social customs)—Juvenile literature.
Classification: LCC HQ801 .M783 2018 | DDC 306.73—dc23
LC record available at https://lccn.loc.gov/2017015073

Printed in the United States of America

Photo Credits: Cover Air Images/Shutterstock.com; p. 5 karelnoppe/Shutterstock.com; p. 8 Voyagerix/Shutterstock.com; p. 12 Hero Images/Getty Images; p. 14 kali9/E+/Getty Images; p. 16 wavebreakmedia/Shutterstock.com; p. 19 Andreas Kuehn/DigitalVision/Getty Images; p. 21 Rob Marmion/Shutterstock.com; p. 22 BFG Images/Getty Images; p. 26 Antonio Guillem/Shutterstock.com; p. 29 John Lund/Marc Romanelli/Blend Images/Getty Images; p. 33 aldomurillo/E+/Getty Images; p. 35 Rob Lewine/Getty Images; p. 37 Petar Chernaev/E+/Getty Images; p. 38 Flying Colours Ltd/Photodisc/Getty Images; p. 41 sirtravelalot/Shutterstock.com; cover and interior pages graphic elements © iStockphoto.com/marigold_88 (waves), Milos Djapovic/Shutttesrock.com (rough texture), Miloje/Shutttesrock.com (circles).

CONTENTS

INTRODUCTION

You've gone through all the emotions and motions of totally crushing on someone: from the butterflies doing battle in your stomach, to the looks across the crowded science lab, to flirting by the lockers and spending hours coming up with witty but not-too-eager texts. Now the moment has come—it's time to be seen in public together. Possibly while eating food.

We dare you not to panic.

The good news is, we've already fought and crawled our way through the perils of dating—kidding! There's tons of fun to be had—and now we're here to help.

Going on your first date is a rite of passage for most of us. It can also be more nerve-wracking than that chemistry final. That's why we've mapped it all out here so that you can prepare for any situation that might arise. Preparation equals confidence and a bigger chance for success—and a second date. (If that's what you want, because you get to decide!)

Kicking your nerves to the curb will help you plan out the best first date of your life. We'll keep you from stressing over something that is supposed to be fun.

Is there food in my teeth? One of a thousand things to think about on your first date.

Going out with your crush is the best way to find out if there's a possibility for a closer relationship. How do you get this done? By doing something away from school and the distractions of your friends, so you can really get to know each other. Also, we've found that flirting really helps lighten the mood. Flirting is fun, and being flirted with is sure to make you feel great.

This book covers it all, from asking your crush out, to planning a great date—and what to do once it's all said and done. Consider this as your total survival guide for all things first date. Are you panicking over asking your crush out? Yep, we've been there and we've got some ideas for you. Worried about being alone together and having absolutely nothing to talk about? We have lots of suggestions so that you can prepare for those potential awkward silences.

We'll tell you absolutely everything we know and we promise not to hold back. We've gathered the best advice and the worst-case scenarios all to give you a successful first date. Whether in a group or one-on-one, we're here for you.

So grab a snack, settle in, and let us tell you how to survive your first date!

CHAPTER ONE

SO YOU WANT TO GO ON A DATE!

You've got a crush and you're ready to make a move. But where to start?

THE BIG ASK

Ready to be bold and ask your crush out on a date? If so, we can give you pointers on being brave! This is a intimidating task, so let's talk about how to ask your maybe-future amore out.

First, and this may seem obvious, but your crush does know you, right? We don't want you to go through all the nervous sweats and anxiety only to have him or her ask, "Sorry, but who are you?" Going on a date means you want to get to know each other better and there's already the possibility of a romantic connection. But if you've only seen your crush in the halls and don't even know his or her last name, maybe pump the brakes on the date concept and get to know your crush at school first. Also, make sure he or she isn't attached to anyone else romantically already. If you've cleared these first hurtles, then let's get ready to move on to the next—the ask.

In all honesty, this is probably the scariest part of the whole thing. Sure, you might be nervous the night of the date, but at least by then you know your date likes you enough to spend more time with you. Start with confidence, even if you have to fake it like a spray can of cheese. Confidence is one of the most attractive qualities in a person and you're already making serious progress just by thinking

Don't wait around for your crush to ask you out. Show off your bravery and do it yourself!

about asking someone out! Just don't act like you're too cool, like you couldn't care less whether your crush says yes or no. You want to appear interested—not like an arrogant jerk.

Now that you've got that confidence, how about adding a dose of bravery? Are you brave enough to do it in person? This will prove your confidence. Facing the one you like is way braver than hiding behind a text or getting a friend to do the asking for you (which can make you look a bit childish and chicken).

When you approach your potential date, try to get to him or her without an audience. You don't need the extra pressure and your crush's friends don't need to watch the whole thing go down. We're guessing (since you like this person) that you know a little bit about his or her schedule. Try to make your approach when your crush is alone—at his or her locker between classes or maybe on the way to his or her car after school. If you can't find your crush at a moment alone, then just ask him or her if the two of you can talk by yourselves for a second.

Definitely lead into your big question instead of pouncing to the point. Build that confidence and get a feel for how your potential date's day is going, too. Start by asking how your crush is doing, how he or she did on the world history test, or if he or she will be playing basketball again this season. Then you can slide in, "Hey, I was wondering. There's this rock-climbing place that I've been dying to check out. Do you want to go with me on Saturday? We could get something to eat afterward." Keep it cool, slightly casual, and full of confidence.

Be clear that this is a date. You don't have to use the word but try to avoid asking if your crush wants to "hang out" Friday night. He or she might be left wondering just what happened; are you two just friends? You don't have to have the date totally planned out in advance, but try to be somewhat specific: "Want to go check out this new restaurant downtown with me on Friday?"

WHAT IF YOUR CRUSH SAYS NO?

First, you deserve a big congrats for going for it. You did a brave thing and have survived to tell the tale. Maybe things didn't work out the way you hoped but now you know where you stand with your (now former?) crush. We know you're wonderful and deserving, but maybe the one you chose just doesn't realize it yet. You went for it, which is more than a lot of people can say. So kudos, for real.

Now? Now it's stiff-upper-lip time, especially if this happened at school or some other public place. Hold back those tears of embarrassment until you make it to the bathroom or an empty classroom—anywhere you can find that's private. Have your moment—it's normal and totally okay—but then try to realize that something really great has happened: The universe has stepped in to tell you that it's not meant to be. You don't have to waste an entire evening with someone who isn't as into you as you are into that person. If he or she had said yes without really feeling it, you'd have sat through hours of forced conversation, wasting time and money. Now, take all your energy and make it a night out with your friends. You'll see, you'll have lots of fun anyway.

WHAT IF YOUR CRUSH SAYS YES?!

The thing you wanted to happen has now happened—you are going on your first date. Yeah!

If you can still feel your face, give your future date a smile! Tell him or her the plan or that you'll text the details later. Exchange phone numbers if you need to. (But make sure you at least have a day agreed upon.)

Now you've got to think about what you want out of the date: To spend a little more time with the person you like? To move your classroom flirting to the next level? To take the first step in becoming a couple? Once you decide how serious you want this date to be, you'll know better how to plan out your date, from something light, such as bike riding, to something a little more formal, such as dinner.

DATE IDEAS THAT TAKE THE PRESSURE OFF

Some people say that the dinner date—although a classic—is the most high-pressure date. It's just the two of you, sitting across from each other with no distractions except the food you must shove in your mouth while looking attractive and coming up with things to talk about. It can be a lot.

So if you're looking for something a little less intimidating, we've got a few suggestions.

Keep it casual and fuss-free with an outdoor date that leaves you close enough for easy flirting.

- Meet up at a coffeehouse for hot chocolate and a pastry (less pressure than a whole meal).
- Hit the movies (a classic date, for sure), then head to out for coffee or dessert—the movie you just saw is a ready-made conversation starter!
- Go hiking or bike riding. Something physical where you don't have to talk or stare at each other the whole time, but still holds the possibility of flirty touching.
- Be do-gooders and volunteer together: serve a meal at a shelter, help out at the animal shelter, or gather clothes or canned goods from the neighbors and donate to a shelter in need.
- Take a cooking class; learn to roll sushi or decorate cakes. Something hands-on with other people around will help make the vibe light and fun.
- Take an arts class, such as painting or pottery-making.

PICK A DATE, ANY DATE— TOGETHER OR ALONE?

When you're a teen, dating can be a one-on-one thing or a group endeavor. There are lots of first date options and for many options you don't have to go as a solo couple. Many people start dating by hanging out in groups. This might blur the lines on if it's truly a date or not, but it's a start and it's way less pressure. Here, we break down the pros and cons of heading out on a date in a group or just the two of you.

13

GROUP DATE

Pros:

- You will fell less pressure to be on the whole night.
- You can rescue yourself from awkward pauses in conversation by talking to others in the group.
- When both friend groups get along, there's a better chance of hanging out again and maybe trying it alone next time.

A supportive group of friends eases the worries of stilted convos and awkward pauses. More friends equals more fun.

- Getting to know your crush's friends tells you a lot about who they are.
- You might realize when you're out with the group that you're actually not as into your crush as you thought.

Cons:

- Friends may accidentally play interference, making it harder to get to know your crush.
- You might end up not liking one of their friends, ruining the vibe of the whole night.
- Your friends might accidentally spill embarrassing details that you'd never want a new crush to know.
- If there are too many people in your group, it might be too hard to get to know your crush.
- The night might end up feeling like nothing more than another Friday night at the football game. In other words, nothing special.

ONE-ON-ONE DATE

Pros:

- There is more potential for romance.
- It's easier to really get to know your date.
- You get your date all to yourself.
- The two of you can choose where to go and what to do instead of negotiating with an entire crowd of friends and opinions.

Movie dates can offer the best of both worlds: you get to be alone together but you don't have the pressure of constant chatter. Bonus points for scary movies—you get to huddle together!

- You don't have to worry what your friends think of your silly jokes or flirty behavior.

Cons:

- All the pressure for conversation is on the two of you.
- It's harder to relax and be yourself, especially if you slip into awkward pauses.

- You can't check in with your friends to see how your date is going.
- If you start babbling or doing that weird laughing thing you do when you get nervous, there's no bestie there to kick you under the table.

No matter what you decide, as long as you stay true to you, you'll do great on your first date!

CHAPTER TWO

GETTING READY: DATE PREP 101

Whatever kind of date you decide upon, there's lots you can do to ensure a great time.

WHAT TO WEAR

What you wear depends on what you're doing and where you're going, obviously. Those high-heeled boots, which are outdoorsy looking, may not be the best shoes to wear if you're going for a hike.

The most important thing to remember when you're getting dressed for a date is to look like yourself. Don't go crazy with tons of makeup, crazily gelled hair, or tight clothes that make you feel (and look) uncomfortable. Your date already likes you for who you are at school—that's the person your date wants to go out with. So be you, but maybe a more cleaned-up version of you. We all know the feeling when the alarm clock screams in the morning and you just can't deal with doing anything extra.

Where am I going, what am I doing, and what do my clothes say about me? The pressures of choosing the perfect outfit.

For your date, though, go for the little extras.

One fun thing you can do is add some scent! Use a strong-scented body wash, or a little roller-ball type of perfume. Just make sure to only use a little bit.

CURB THE NERVES

Being nervous before a date is totally natural. In fact, your date is probably just as nervous as you are. Nerves are normal. Your date probably feels the pressure too! But guess what? Even if you feel like everything you say or do sounds stupid or weird, you're probably acting normal!

"I have learned that often times when you think you are being awkward it is all in your head, and the other person doesn't really notice or think anything of it," said recent high school grad Sidney K.

Keep calm and carry on despite a battle of the butterflies with these easy tips:

- Rock the endorphins pre-date by exercising. Go for a run, power walk through the neighborhood, or have your friends join you in some power yoga (you can find lots of free sessions on YouTube).
- Talk to your friends. That's easy, right? Tell them why you're nervous and let their kind words help you see that you'll be fine and the night will be great.
- Make sure you know what the plan is. Sometimes your date will pick you up with no plans for the evening. "Whatever you want to do," they might say.

Zen for the win. Curb your nerves and wake up your endorphins with a day-of-date workout! (Just remember to shower afterward.)

It's happened. And frankly it's annoying because then all the pressure is on you to, you know, plan the date on the spot. Whoever did the asking out should share the plans for the night ahead of time so everyone is clear on what's happening. If your date won't tell you the plans because "it's a surprise," at least find out how you should dress. You don't want to be stuck freezing at an outdoor concert because you wore a thin T-shirt.

A LITTLE SOMETHING SPECIAL

Shower and brush those teeth. We know—duh. But you don't want to smell like the soccer field you just came from or the

coffee you just guzzled. Wear clean clothes, don't grab something from the hamper (or floor) and throw it on. If you're wearing jeans, go for one of your nicer, less ripped, and faded pair. You want to show your date you care enough to put a little extra effort in. If you need it, go for a clean, fresh shave before heading out. Maybe even consider bumping up your accessory game. A little sparkle goes a long way.

Being on top of your pre-date prep will make you feel confident—which looks good on everybody.

- If you're meeting there, leave plenty of time to get ready and arrive on time. Being late is rude and gives the impression that you don't care. Rushing also totally amps up your stress level.
- Try to let go. If you're tense, your date will feel tense. Leave home knowing that everything might not go perfectly, but that you'll still probably have fun anyway! Your date will also pick up on that energy. And know that if the date doesn't go well, you'll have a different kind of story to tell your friends!

PACK AND GO

Before you head out, make sure you prepare a few things with you just in case:

- Some cash and a loaded debit card (either to pay your own way, pay for both of you, or if you need an emergency ride home)
- Fully charged cell phone
- A backup ride in case you need someone else to take you home
- Breath mints
- Tickets or reservation number, if relevant
- An open attitude to a fun tonight!

LEAVE IT AT HOME

We bet you can live without these things for one evening:

- An arsenal of makeup. Yes, you want to look your best and discreetly refreshing your lip gloss is okay, but steadily reapplying the whole war paint all night is annoying and distracting for you both. Put your best face forward before you leave home and know that your date probably asked you out when you were wearing less (makeup, that is!).
- Diet restrictions. If you've got a nut or gluten allergy, obviously stick to that. We don't want to see you break out in hives or go into anaphylactic shock on your date. But if you're trying out a new juice cleanse or raw diet, maybe hit pause on it for the evening.
- The tight, short dress or the too-high heels that pinch your feet even though you look *ah*-mazing in them. You want to look your best—we get it—but it's hard to look great when you're in pain.
- A bad attitude. Definitely leave this one at home! Head out thinking of all the positives that might come out of this date.

CHAPTER THREE

IT'S GO TIME!

t's finally happening! Your very first date! You're prepped, dressed, and out on the town. So ...

WHAT ARE YOU GOING TO TALK ABOUT?

Conversation is one of the things that worries people the most. What are we going to talk about? What if there are long awkward silences? What if my date thinks I'm boring? What if I say something weird? What if my jokes are lame? We've made it easier for you with prompts and suggestions to keep the words coming.

DO ask about the person. A date is to get to know someone you like on a deeper level.

DON'T talk about some other person you once liked.

DO ask fun, light questions. Ask your date how sports

Use your words! Talking is the best way to get to know your date. Ask questions about your date's likes and dislikes—and don't forget to listen to the answers.

practice is going, or when he or she started playing guitar; or more general stuff like what your date's all-time favorite movie is, what's the first concert he or she ever went to, or where your date would live if he or she could pick anywhere in the world.

DON'T put your own interests or abilities down to make your date feel better.

DO listen when your date talks, and make eye contact.

DON'T feel like you have to talk over every pause in

conversation. They happen! A pause doesn't mean your date is bored or that the outing is turning into a disaster.

DINNER DOS & DON'TS

The dinner date is a classic, so make sure you don't treat your evening meal like afternoon pizza with your buds. Remember, you're here to elevate your relationship with this person you like. Here are a few reminders to get through dinner with lots of grace and confidence.

DO have good table manners. Napkin in lap, chew with your mouth closed—you know, the basics you learned when you were a kid.

DO consider checking out the menu ahead of time so you can think about what you might order and what sort of options are on the menu (including prices). That way you won't be surprised and you'll have time to think uninterrupted about what you might want to eat (especially if it turns out only one or two things sounds appetizing).

DON'T feel like you have to order the cheapest thing on the menu ("I'll just have a cup of soup"). You also don't need to go for the priciest—unless you're definitely paying, that is. Get what you want, but try not to break the bank.

DO share your food. Offer your date a taste, and if you're feeling bold and flirty, feed him or her from your fork.

DON'T be rude to the waiter, even if the waiter messes up your order, and take note if your date does. You can learn

27

a lot about your date by watching how they treat someone whose job it is to serve you.

DO flirt if you're feeling it! Hopefully you're in this situation because you like each other so we say go for it!

DON'T take it too seriously. It's just dinner!

WHO PAYS?

The moment the bill arrives (if you're at a restaurant, for example) can be uncomfortable. Do you feel like you should pay your own way? Should you pay for yourself? What are the rules?

A good rule of thumb is that whoever proposed the date should pay. If you didn't propose the date but feel strongly that you want to contribute, offer to pay half. Alternatively, if you're going somewhere next, such as a movie, say you'll get the tickets. Even if your date insists on paying you'll feel better for offering. Even better? If the date went well, tell him or her that the next time is on you. And don't forget to say thank you!

(DON'T) HOLD THE PHONE: SOCIAL MEDIA ETIQUETTE

We know that, technically speaking and with no exaggeration whatsoever, your phone is an extension of your hand, your personality, and your reason for breathing.

Old-fashioned rules are just that—old-fashioned! Whoever asks the other out should pay. Equality is sexy!

It's how you communicate with the world, entertain and inform yourself, keep up with your friends, and show the world what you're up to. You can't live without it. We wouldn't want you to.

But let's be honest: phones can be a distraction. They can also be a shield. We've all hidden behind the glare of our phones when we get bored. What signal does it send when you're looking at your phone instead of your date? It says that whatever is on your phone is more interesting than your date is.

Your hand might itch to grab onto it when the conversation slows (or slams to a dead stop), but try to resist. Gaps in conversation are not the death knell of the evening. Just because you're not speaking for every single second of the night doesn't mean you're totally incompatible and the night is a wash. Pause your panic and let the moment slip by without using your phone as a crutch. Because honestly, it's kind of unattractive to be more engrossed in your phone than your date.

As much as it might physically pain you, refrain from texting, tweeting, posting, liking, and snapping while you're on your date. When you go for your phone, your date will be more likely to go for his or hers as well. And how lame is it to be on a date with someone really cute when you're not even looking at or talking to each other? You might as well be sitting alone in your bedroom.

EYES UP!

According to Stopphubbing.com, 87 percent of teens would rather communicate via text than face to face. But we bet you don't want to text your date from across the dinner table, right?

That's not to say there's never an okay time to use your phone on a date. Maybe you need the flashlight to see in the dark or maybe you're having a conversation about how your shared friend once met her favorite actor and you have a photo on your phone. If you're having a great time together and you both want to snap a pic, then great! Save the posting for later (and ask if it's okay first) and get back to having fun. Instagram will still be there when you get home.

WHEN BAD DATES HAPPEN TO GOOD PEOPLE

Even the best-laid plans can go wrong. You can't guarantee a date will go perfectly. If things don't work out, don't blame yourself. You could have a bad date because of any number of innocent reasons: nerves (your date's, yours, or both), a bad choice in restaurant or a terrible movie, or even just lousy weather.

It won't seem like it at the time, but bad dates can be good things. You'll have a funny story to tell your friends. And you might even have some pretty good dating don'ts that you can avoid next time.

Remember that your date is probably secretly nervous and freaking out, too. He or she is also worried about the conversation, being funny enough, or that the place is lame. So if things are going wrong, but you're not ready to bail, take deep breaths and give the evening—and your date—a chance.

Beyond that? If you feel like something is totally off and you're not comfortable—or if your date is being rude—you can always end the date early

EXIT STRATEGY: GETTING OUT SAFELY IF THINGS GO WRONG

What if your date turns more heinous than you ever could have imagined? If you're feeling unsafe, remember that you are the priority—not your date's feelings or what he or she might say about you. "An escape plan for a date is always a good idea," says Jeana M. Hill, a therapist who works with kids, teens, and families. "You never want to feel trapped." Here are some get-out-quick tips:

Before you even leave, make sure your parents know where you're going. If plans change mid-evening, text to let them know.

Listen to your gut. You know when things are taking a wrong turn—you can feel that icky, don't-want-it-to-be-true pit in the bottom of your stomach. If you listen to your gut early enough, you can leave the date with a little white lie of not feeling well.

Be honest. If your date is being a jerk, don't be afraid to stand up for yourself and tell him or her you're uncomfortable or that you're leaving.

If things go wrong and you feel unsafe with your date, waste no time in calling a friend or parent to come get you. Always listen to your gut— and never feel guilty about doing so!

If your date gets drunk, grabs you, or does anything else that falls under "oh, hell no," slip off to the restroom and call your parents or friend to come get you stat. You don't even need to tell your date. He or she doesn't deserve it.

If you're feeling red-level unsafe, go to an adult who works wherever you are and ask them to help you. Ask if this adult can stay with you until your alternate ride arrives. Stay in the bathroom or ask the manager if you can wait in the office if you're afraid to face your date.

KISS, KISS, MISS, MISS

Are you ready for the physical part of dating? For some of us it's the most nerve-wracking. Is my date going to try to kiss me? Do I want them to?

Here come the lips! It's happening. It's the end of the night and your date is leaning in toward you with lips half open and eyes half closed. Your heart is racing. What are you going to do?!

If you've got a case of the nerves or you aren't feeling it yet, turn a sly cheek when your date comes in for the kiss. You can sweetly tell him or her that you're just not ready, but you do like him or her and hope you can go out again and continue to get to know each other. Your date should respect this without giving you any pressure to push forward.

What if your date doesn't take your rebuff so gently? Time for you to get firm and tell him or her to slow down

Mwah! A little kiss on the cheek is sweet, but go slow and respect your date's boundaries.

or back off. This does not make you rude. It keeps you in control.

"No one has the right to enter your personal space without your permission, and no one has the right to touch you unless you allow it," says Ms. Hill. "Someone who truly likes you and wants to have a relationship with you will not disrespect your boundaries."

CHAPTER FOUR

YOU DATED! NOW WHAT?

It's over. Congratulations! You had your first date and survived to tell the tale! Now you can get on with the rest of your life. But what happens now? What if you go home at the end of the evening and you're not sure if it went well? Does he or she still like me? Did I make a fool of myself? Will this person ever want to see me again?

Let the over-analysis begin! For many of us, it's inevitable. Gather your friends and go over all the details of the night, from whether or not your date laughed at that joke you and all your buddies love, to spilling the details of how loud he or she screamed in that scary part of the movie.

It'll feel good to get it out all out and relive the night, whether it was good or bad. Let your friends comfort or build you up. But make sure the decision on how the night truly went is based on your own experience and not clouded by what others might think.

Lean on your friends post-date for support...and to go over every detail of the outing!

HOW TO HANDLE THE NEXT DAY—AND SCHOOL

Let's just assume your date was a success. Hooray! Now what?! Here are our tips on ensuring you'll get that second date—without playing those dating games.

First up, we truly believe that the waiting game is silly. There no rules on how long you have to wait to hit up your date online or via text. If you had a great time, send a text the next day. It doesn't mean you're desperate, it means you had a good time. You can make a reference to last night ("I keep thinking about our weird waiter. Can't believe he spilled your drink!") or just let your date know you had fun ("Had so much fun last night. We should do it again sometime.") or that you appreciated him or her taking you

Did you have fun with your date? Here's an idea: tell her so! Talk to your date at school—and maybe even flirt a little.

out ("Thanks for such a fun night! Next time is on me"). As long as the texting goes back and forth, it's fine. But if you find yourself texting long blocks and only getting two-word responses, it's time to ease up.

You can consider asking if your date wants to meet up before school and walk to class together. Or drop by his or her locker between classes. You don't have to stick together all day long but popping back in to spend a little time together is an easy transition from a great date.

Maybe even ask your date if he or she wants to sit together at lunch later in the week. You don't have to start strong on Monday, but a mini-date mid-week might be a good way to be with your date and your friends at the same time.

Keep in mind that even if the date went well, that doesn't mean you're an instant couple. You both still need to go step by step—texting a little more, hanging out at school together, going on a second date—before you both agree that you are an exclusive couple.

WHAT IF YOUR FRIENDS DON'T LIKE YOUR DATE?

No matter how your date went, everyone's probably got an opinion on the two of you—especially your friends. And what if they don't like your date? This is a tricky one, so we went straight to a pro to answer this one.

"First, do you trust your friends? How well do you know [your date]?" asks Ms. Hill. "[Your friends] may know about behaviors from [your crush] that you don't. Often, we are blinded by our emotions and don't notice red flags. If there are no jealousy issues between your friends and they [are] genuinely [concerned], finding out why they don't like [this person] may help you at least have your eyes open … and notice red flags when they pop up."

Be prepared to find out something about your date that you didn't know and that you don't like. Maybe your date has hit on some of your friends. Maybe they've been rude or disrespectful to them or someone they know. Maybe they've got a girlfriend or boyfriend at another school. Or maybe your friend who's warning you likes your date. Who knows! Maybe your date is just really quiet in certain situations and your friends read that as snobbery. The point is, listen to your friends' side of things first.

Once you've done all that, listen to your gut. Is your date a good person? Did he or she treat you well? Was he or she kind? That's what's important. That's also what a first date is for—to find out more about this person so you can form your own opinion. Maybe your date's personality simply clashes with one of your friends' and it's nothing more than that. But your friends could be right, too. It's up to you to listen to all the signs and decide for yourself.

BETTER OFF FRIENDS?

Your date might have gone perfectly fine, no real problems or complaints. But there's one thing missing—the spark. And that spark is what separates friends from boy and girlfriends.

A friendship can turn into a romantic relationship, but if the vibes aren't happening on your first date that's a bad sign for future fireworks. You might be better off as friends if:

New couple alert? Maybe your date was a success and you're ready for something more. If not, know that you'll find someone special soon.

- Your date brings up other people you know and ask questions like, "Do you know if she's dating anyone?" (Also, rude.)
- Your date keeps calling you his or her friend.
- You both keep your physical distance all night long. Going at your own pace is one thing; shrinking away from even an accidental hand brush signals lack of romantic interest.
- Your date couldn't get out of the car fast enough at the end of the night or you checked the time on your phone a hundred times.
- Your date puts off going on another date, but still asks you to help with his or her calculus homework.
- Your date brings a friend on the first date. Maybe he or she didn't know it was a date, or maybe you've been friend-zoned before the night even started!

SOCIAL STRATEGY

After the date, ask if it's okay for you to post that you were out together. It's a nice courtesy that shows you care about your date's boundaries. Maybe he or she is not ready to tell the world you've been out together. That's not a diss on you; it might just mean your date wants to go a bit slower and hold off on the public declaration of dating. It's important that you respect that.

YOU DID IT!

You made it! Your first date is said and done. All the little things you worried about have come to pass and your first date is in your rearview mirror. Good or bad, take a few lessons from it and put it in your back pocket. Guess what? There will be more first dates in your life. Some will be great, some not-so-much, and one or two might change your life. We hope we've helped ease some of the anxiety now that you have survived your first date!

GLOSSARY

arsenal A stock or store of items saved for later.

boundaries Something defining a limit or end, like a line.

courtesy A favor performed in a kind and thoughtful fashion.

discreet Showing good judgment, especially in what you say and how you behave.

endeavor To try, to work toward a particular goal.

endorphin Chemical in your body, especially your brain, that scientists believe can help you to feel good and relieve pain.

exclusive Sole or only. In relationships, this means you are dating only one person.

foolproof Something made or organized so simply nothing can go wrong.

intimidate To scare someone, possibly by being threatening.

inevitable Definitely going to happen.

negotiate To talk something over with someone in hopes of coming to an agreement.

over-analysis To examine a topic too closely or for too long.

transition A change from one state to another, could be physical or emotional.

FURTHER READING

BOOKS

Corinna, Heather. *S.E.X.: The All-You-Need-to-Know Sexuality Guide to Get Through Your Teens and Twenties*. 2nd ed. Boston, MA: Da Capo Lifelong Books, 2016.

Lang, Amy. *Dating Smarts: What Every Teen Needs to Know to Date, Relate or Wait!* CreateSpace, 2016.

Langford, Jo. *Spare Me 'The Talk!': A Guy's Guide to Sex, Relationships, and Growing Up*. Mercer Island, WA: Parent Map, 2015.

Langford, Jo. *Spare Me 'The Talk!': A Girl's Guide to Sex, Relationships, and Growing Up*. Mercer Island, WA: Parent Map, 2016.

WEBSITES

Channel One

www.channelone.com

Keep up with news that's relevant to you (and possible topics of conversation on your date).

Girl Zone

www.girlzone.com

A community for teen girls that provides articles and advice on everything from health to friendship and fashion fun.

Young Men's Health

www.youngmenshealthsite.org

Tackles issues from embarrassing health questions to dealing with girls and parents.

INDEX